The Basilica of the Sacréd Heart of Paris: The Hi Sacré-Cœur

By Charles River Editors

Alexander Migl's picture of the gable above the main entrance

About Charles River Editors

Charles River Editors is a boutique digital publishing company, specializing in bringing history back to life with educational and engaging books on a wide range of topics. Keep up to date with our new and free offerings with this 5 second sign up on our weekly mailing list, and visit Our Kindle Author Page to see other recently published Kindle titles.

We make these books for you and always want to know our readers' opinions, so we encourage you to leave reviews and look forward to publishing new and exciting titles each week.

Introduction

A picture of the basilica from the Arc de Triomphe

"Glorious servant of God, St. Denis, with intense love did you devote yourself to Christ after learning to know Him through the apostle St. Paul. Preaching His saving name to the nations, and bringing the knowledge and love of God, for Who's sake you did not shrink from martyrdom..." – The Invocation of St. Denis

Perched atop a bed of luxuriant grass on the Montmartre crest, the highest hilltop in the 18th arrondissement of Paris, stands a princely, cream-white monument known around the world as the Sacré-Cœur Basilica. An estimated 10 million visitors hike up the 300 steps to this iconic landmark each year, and on a good year, this figure rises to anywhere between 11.5 and 12 million people. Half of those who make the difficult, but worthwhile journey to the Sacré-Cœur are pilgrims, eager to gaze upon the breathtaking Christ in Majesty mosaic and receive the Eucharist from the blessed tabernacle of the Sacréd Heart. The others mostly consist of tourists, many of them drawn to the unique silhouette and exquisite elegance of the basilica that has become one of the French capital's most notable landmarks.

The Basilica of the Sacréd Heart of Paris: The History and Legacy of the Sacré-Cœur looks at the architectural history of the site, the events that inspired its creation, and the scandals that continue to surround it to this day. Along with pictures depicting important people, places, and events, you will learn about the Sacré-Cœur like never before.

Montmartre and the Druids

Christophe Meneboeuf's picture of Montmartre

Those who erected the legendary architectural gem affectionately referred to as the "Alabaster Wedding Cake" and the "Taj Mahal of France," now the most visited place of worship in the entire nation after the damage done to Notre-Dame, were indeed visionaries, but they were far from pioneers. In fact, the hallowed hilltop of Montmartre, where the Sacré-Cœur Basilica now stands, has been hailed as Sacréd grounds for over 1,000 years.

In antiquity, Paris was devoid of the charming bistros, bustling souvenir shops, delightful artisanal markets, cobblestone paths, cement roads, leaving a sparsely populated area. The hilltop that is now home to the Sacré-Cœur Basilica was a lush, fertile mound surrounded by clusters of round houses with thatched straw roofs. The isolation and height of this steep hill, which towered over the emerging village at 430 feet, already made it the ideal place of prayer given its apparent proximity to the heavens. Moreover, whenever the sun greeted and bade its farewell to the village's inhabitants each day, it lingered behind the hilltop, and though it was just for a few moments, the crest of the mound was illuminated by a halo of light, as if the heavens were shining a spotlight directly on it.

The potential importance of this then-unoccupied hilltop was not lost on the ancient Gauls who lived in this area. The Druids of the village, an educated and honorable Celtic class of nature-lovers that consisted of teachers, magicians, priests, judges, and oracles, are now believed to be among the first to lay claim to the hilltop and, more significantly, attach spiritual meaning to it.

Naturally, people have been interested in Druids for centuries mostly because they don't understand much about the Druids or their practices. The word comes from the Romans, who labeled them "Druidae" in reference to the white robed order of Celtic priests living in Gaul, Britain, and Ireland. They were a well-organized, secretive group who kept no written records and performed their rituals - allegedly including human sacrifice - in oaken groves, all of which interested and horrified Roman writers. As Pliny wrote in the 1st century CE, "Barbarous rites were found in Gaul even within my own memory. For it was then that the emperor Tiberius passed a decree through the senate outlawing their Druids and these types of diviners and physicians. But why do I mention this about a practice which has crossed the sea and reached the ends of the earth? For even today Britain performs rites with such ceremony that you would think they were the source for the extravagant Persians. It is amazing how distant people are so similar in such practices. But at least we can be glad that the Romans have wiped out the murderous cult of the Druids, who thought human sacrifice and ritual cannibalism were the greatest kind of piety."

People love reading about the Druids, yet many would have a hard time even defining them, and there is even considerable debate about the etymology of the word "Druid." The first steps of this word are relatively clear: "Druid" in English comes from "Druide" in French (perhaps in the 1560s), and this comes from the Latin "Druidae", which was the term used by the ancient Roman chroniclers. However, the more interesting and useful question is what is the origin of the term in Latin. Did the chroniclers invent the word, or was it borrowed from some Gaulish or other Celtic terminology? If the latter is true, than understanding the origins of "Druidae" may explain how the ancient Celts saw their religious leaders, much the same way insights can be gained from analyzing the Christian title "pastor," which is drawn from the term for someone who cares for a flock of animals and says something about the ways that early Christians viewed their spiritual leaders.

Unfortunately, the modern Celtic languages do not provide much help, because their terms for Druids are typically borrowed from English, as with the Cornish word "drewyth ("drewydhyon" for the plural).[1] However, for over a century, scholars have examined the extant Celtic tongues and compared them to the written fragments of earlier incarnations to attempt to reconstruct a language they call Old Celtic, and by examining the hypothetical words of Old Celtic (for which there are no written records), scholars can propose theories of the origins of words like "Druidae."

It is from the written record, specifically the writings of Roman chroniclers, that people first learned about the Druids, and ultimately it is from these important but questionable sources that scholars have the only confirmed evidence about the beliefs and practices of the ancient Druids.

---

1   In Nance's classic 1952 *A New Cornish Dictionary* (pg 43), the term is further attributed from borrowing from Welsh and Breton.

Even before the rise of the Roman Empire, ancient historians described the Celts and some of their rituals. According to the ancient Greek historian Athenaeus, in the 4th century BCE, Sopater noted, "Among them is the custom, whenever they are victorious in battle, to sacrifice their prisoners to the gods. So I, like the Celts, have vowed to the divine powers to burn those three false dialecticians as an offering." In the early 3rd century BCE, Timaeus wrote, "Historians point out that the Celts who live on the shore of the Ocean honor the Dioscori above other gods. For there is an ancient tradition among them that these gods came to them from the Ocean."

Another Greek historian noted their use of sacrifices, "Eudoxus says that the Celts do the following (and if anyone thinks his account credible, let him believe it; if not, let him ignore it). When clouds of locusts invade their country and damage the crops, the Celts evoke certain prayers and offer sacrifices which charm birds—and the birds hear these prayers, come in flocks, and destroy the locusts. If however one of them should capture one of these birds, his punishment according to the laws of the country is death. If he is pardoned and released, this throws the birds into a rage, and to revenge the captured bird they do not respond if they are called on again." Strabo noted a similar anecdote: "The following story which Artemidorus has told about the crows is unbelievable. There is a certain harbor on the coast which, according to him, is named 'Two Crows'. In this harbor are seen two crows, with their right wings somewhat white. Men who are in dispute about certain matters come here, put a plank on an elevated place, and then each man separately throws up cakes of barley. The birds fly up and eat some of the cakes, but scatter others. The man whose cakes are scattered wins the dispute. Although this story is implausible, his report about the goddesses Demeter and Core is more credible. He says that there is an island near Britain on which sacrifices are performed like those in Samothrace for Demeter and Core."

Ultimately, the most concrete descriptions of the Druids came from several Roman writers, who offer tantalizing glimpses into the lost religious and ritual world of the Druids and overwhelmingly demonstrate the social power that the Druids had and the ways that Romans seemed to often hold them in awe as well.

Perhaps the most detailed discussion of the Druids and their ways comes from Julius Caesar's *Notebooks About the Gallic War*, which discusses Celtic society and the Druids at length:

> "Throughout Gaul there are two classes of persons of definite account and dignity…Of the two classes above mentioned one consists of Druids, the other of knights. The former are concerned with divine worship, the due performance of sacrifices, public and private, and the interpretation of ritual questions: a great number of young men gather about them for the sake of instruction and hold them in great honour.

> "A great many young men come to the Druids for instruction, holding them in great respect. Indeed, the Druids are the judges on all controversies public and

private. If any crime has been committed, if any murder done, if there are any questions concerning inheritance, or any controversy concerning boundaries, the Druids decide the case and determine punishments. If anyone ignores their decision, that person is banned from all sacrifices—an extremely harsh punishment among the Gauls. Those who are so condemned are considered detestable criminals. Everyone shuns them and will not speak with them, fearing some harm from contact with them, and they receive no justice nor honor for any worthy deed.

"Among all the Druids there is one who is the supreme leader, holding highest authority over the rest. When the chief Druid dies, whoever is the most worthy succeeds him. If there are several of equal standing, a vote of all the Druids follows, though the leadership is sometimes contested even by armed force. At a certain time of the year, all the Druids gather together at a consecrated spot in the territory of the Carnutes, whose land is held to be the center of all Gaul. Everyone gathers therefrom the whole land to present disputes and they obey the judgments and decrees of the Druids. It is said that the Druidic movement began in Britain and was then carried across to Gaul. Even today, those who wish to study their teachings most diligently usually travel to Britain.

"The Druids are exempt from serving in combat and from paying war taxes, unlike all other Gauls. Tempted by such advantages, many young people willingly commit themselves to Druidic studies while others are sent by their parents. It is said that in the schools of the Druids they learn a great number of verses, so many in fact that some students spend twenty years in training. It is not permitted to write down any of these Sacréd teachings, though other public and private transactions are often recorded in Greek letters. I believe they practice this oral tradition for two reasons: first, so that the common crowd does not gain access to their secrets and second, to improve the faculty of memory. Truly, writing does often weaken one's diligence in learning and reduces the ability to memorize. The cardinal teaching of the Druids is that the soul does not perish, but after death passes from one body to another. Because of this teaching that death is only a transition, they are able to encourage fearlessness in battle. They have a great many other teachings as well which they hand down to the young concerning such things as the motion of the stars, the size of the cosmos and the earth, the order of the natural world, and the power of the immortal gods.

"All of the Gauls are greatly devoted to religion, and because of this those who are afflicted with terrible illnesses or face dangers in battle will conduct human sacrifices, or at least vow to do so. The Druids are the ministers at such occasions. They believe that unless the life of a person is offered for the life of another, the dignity of the immortal gods will be insulted. This is true both in private and public sacrifices. Some build enormous figures which they fill with living persons and then set on fire, everyone perishing inflames. They believe that the execution of thieves and other criminals is the most pleasing to the gods, but, when the supply of guilty persons runs short, they will kill the innocent as well.

"The chief god of the Gauls is Mercury and there are images of him everywhere. He is said to be the inventor of all the arts, the guide for every road and journey, and the most influential god in trade and moneymaking. After him, they worship Apollo, Mars, Jupiter, and Minerva. These gods have the same areas of influence as among most other peoples. Apollo drives away diseases, Minerva is most influential in crafts, Jupiter rules the sky, and Mars is the god of war. Before a great battle, they will often dedicate the spoils to Mars. If they are successful, they will sacrifice all the living things they have captured and other spoils they gather together in one place. Among many tribes, you can see these spoils placed together in a Sacréd spot. And it is a very rare occasion that anyone would dare to disturb these valuable goods and conceal them in his home. If it does happen, the perpetrator is tortured and punished in the worst ways imaginable.

"The Gauls all say that they are descended from the god of the dark underworld, Dis, and confirm that this is the teaching of the Druids. Because of this they measure time by the passing of nights, not days. Birthdays and the beginnings of months and years all start at night.

"The funerals of the Gauls are magnificent and extravagant. Everything which was dear to the departed is thrown into the fire, including animals. In the recent past, they would also burn faithful slaves and beloved subordinates at the climax of the funeral."[2]

Caesar, while writing something of a puff-piece in *Notebooks*, certainly had firsthand knowledge of the Druids from his time fighting the Gauls and was thus an invaluable direct observer. While probably writing from second-hand sources, Strabo gave a similar description of the Druids' high status in his seminal *Geography*, which was published in the first decade of the 1st century BCE, before Caesar's work: "Among all the Gallic peoples, generally speaking, there are three sets of men who are held in exceptional honour; the Bards, the Vates and the Druids. The Bards are singers and poets; the Vates, diviners and natural philosophers; while the Druids, in addition to natural philosophy, study also moral philosophy."[3]

While these theological points may have been of some interest to the Romans, one area of

---

2   All of the Caesar quotes are from: *The Gallic War* by Julius Caesar, Book VI Chapters 13-14. Accessed online at: http://penelope.uchicago.edu/Thayer/E/Roman/Texts/Caesar/Gallic_War/6B*.html#13

3   All of the Strabo quotes come from *The Geography Book IV, Chapter 4:4* accessed online at: http://penelope.uchicago.edu/Thayer/E/Roman/Texts/Strabo/4D*.html#4.4

religious practice that always intrigued ancient writers was divination: the ability to tell the future or of far off events. The famous Roman orator and philosopher Cicero described the Druids, amongst the religious practitioners of several foreign peoples, in his work *De Divinatione* (*"Of Divination"*). He wrote in approximately 44 BCE, "Nor is the practice of divination disregarded even among uncivilized tribes, if indeed there are Druids in Gaul — and there are, for I knew one of them myself, Divitiacus, the Aeduan, your guest and eulogist. He claimed to have that knowledge of nature which the Greeks call 'physiologia,' and he used to make predictions, sometimes by means of augury and sometimes by means of conjecture."[4] Strabo also mentioned Druidic divination: "They used to strike a human being, whom they had devoted to death, in the back with a sabre, and then divine from his death-struggle. But they would not sacrifice without the Druids."[5]

Of course, the Druids' abstinence from warfare and religious tributes, as well as their practice of lawful tax evasion, were also tempting incentives. Those in the Montmartre neighborhood were vested with magisterial powers, most notably the ability to determine the verdict of disputes, whether personal or public, and the right to dole out punishments. Among the slew of reportedly cruel and unusual punishment imposed upon Celtic lawbreakers, which included being sewn into a sack and tossed into the surging river, was sacrificial prohibition. Stripping a civilian of the right to attend or partake in sacrificial ceremonies, they say, was the most dreadful penalty that could befall a Gaul.

Diodorus Sicilus described Druidic rituals surrounding divination at length:

"The Gauls have certain wise men and experts on the gods called Druids, as well as a highly respected class of seers. Through auguries and animal sacrifice these seers predict the future and no one dares to scoff at them. They have an especially odd and unbelievable method of divination for the most important matters. Having anointed a human victim, they stab him with a small knife in the area above the diaphragm. When the man has collapsed from the wound, they interpret the future by observing the nature of his fall, the convulsion of his limbs, and especially from the pattern of his spurting blood. In this type of divination, the seers place great trust in an ancient tradition of observation.

"It is a custom among the Gauls to never perform a sacrifice without someone skilled in divine ways present. They say that those who know about the nature of the gods should offer thanks to them and make requests of them, as though these people spoke the same language as the gods. The Gauls, friends and foes alike, obey the rule of the priests and bards not only in time of peace but also during wars. It

---

4   *De Divinatione* Book I 41:90, accessed online at:
    http://penelope.uchicago.edu/Thayer/E/Roman/Texts/Cicero/de_Divinatione/1*.html
5   Strabo's *The Geography Book IV, Chapter 4:5*

has often happened that just as two armies approached each other with swords drawn and spears ready, the Druids will step between the two sides and stop the fighting, as if they had cast a spell on wild beasts. Thus even among the wildest barbarians, anger yields to wisdom and the god of war respects the Muses…

"It is in keeping with their wildness and savage nature that they carry out particularly offensive religious practices. They will keep some criminal under guard for five years, then impale him on a pole in honor of their gods—followed by burning him on an enormous pyre along with many other first-fruits. They also use prisoners of war as sacrifices to the gods. Some of the Gauls will even sacrifice animals captured in war, either by slaying them, burning them, or by killing them with some other type of torture."

A better-known account of their divinatory and magical practices comes from *The Natural History*, by Pliny the Elder, who mentions the Druids in his chapter on mistletoe. He noted:

"I can't forget to mention the admiration the Gauls have for mistletoe. The Druids (which is the name of their holy men) hold nothing more sacred than this plant and the tree on which it grows—as if it grew only on oaks. They worship only in oak groves and will perform no sacred rites unless a branch of that tree is present. It seems the Druids even get their name from drus (the Greek word for oak). And indeed they think that anything which grows on an oak tree is sent from above and is a sign that the tree was selected by the god himself. The problem is that in fact mistletoe rarely grows on oak trees. Still they search it out with great diligence and then will cut it only on the sixth day of the moon's cycle, because the moon is then growing in power but is not yet halfway through its course (they use the moon to measure not only months but years and their grand cycle of thirty years). In their language they call mistletoe a name meaning "all-healing". They hold sacrifices and sacred meals under oak trees, first leading forward two white bulls with horns bound for the first time. A priest dressed in white then climbs the tree and cuts the mistletoe with a golden sickle, with the plant dropping onto a white cloak. They then sacrifice the bulls while praying that the god will favorably grant his own gift to those to whom he has given it. They believe a drink made with mistletoe will restore fertility to barren livestock and act as a remedy to all poisons. Such is the devotion to frivolous affairs shown by many peoples.

"Similar to the Sabine herb savin is a plant called selago. It must be picked without an iron instrument by passing the right hand through the opening of the left sleeve, as if you were stealing it. The harvester, having first offered bread and wine, must wear white and have clean, bare feet. It is carried in a new piece of cloth. The Druids of Gaul say that it is should be used to ward off every danger and that the smoke of burning selago is good for eye diseases. The Druids also gather a plant from marshes called samolus, which must be picked with the left hand during a time of fasting. It is good for the diseases of cows, but the one who gathers it must not look back nor place it anywhere except in the watering trough of the animals.

"There is a kind of egg which is very famous in Gaul but ignored by Greek writers. In the summer months, a vast number of snakes will gather themselves together in a ball which is held together by their saliva and a secretion from their bodies. The Druids say they produce this egg-like object called an anguinum which the hissing snakes throw up into the air. It must be caught, so they say, in a cloak before it hits the ground. But you'd better have a horse handy, because the snakes will chase you until they are cut off by some stream. A genuine anguinum will float upstream, even if covered in gold. But as is common with the world's holy men, the Druids say it can only be gathered during a particular phase of the moon, as if people could make the moon and serpents work together. I saw one of these eggs myself—it was a small round thing like an apple with a hard surface full of indentations as on the arms of an octopus. The Druids value them highly. They say it is a great help in lawsuits and will help you gain the good will of a ruler. That this is plainly false is shown by a man of the Gaulish Vocontii tribe, a Roman knight, who kept one hidden in his cloak during a trial before the emperor Claudius and was executed, as far as I can tell, for this reason alone.

"Barbarous rites were found in Gaul even within my own memory. For it was then that the emperor Tiberius passed a decree through the senate outlawing their Druids and these types of diviners and physicians. But why do I mention this about a practice which has crossed the sea and reached the ends of the earth? For even today Britain performs rites with such ceremony that you would think they were the source for the extravagant Persians. It is amazing how distant people are so similar in such practices. But at least we can be glad that the Romans have wiped out the murderous cult of the Druids, who thought human sacrifice and ritual cannibalism were the greatest kind of piety."[6]

In this excerpt, Pliny offers perhaps the richest detail of all of the ancient sources. His account includes details of Druidic ritual - the use of oak groves, the importance of mistletoe - that were not noted anywhere else, and it's perhaps no coincidence that worship in oaken groves was not unique to the Druids, as there is evidence that the Germanic god Thor/Donar was worshiped primarily in this context as well.[7]

One of the most important observations that emerges from the Roman accounts is that the

---

6   *Natural History* by Pliny the Elder, Volume 3, Book XVI: Chapter 95
7   *Thor: The Origins, History and Evolution of the Norse God* by Jesse Harasta (2013). Charles River Editors.

Druids had two distinct roles within society, making it all but impossible to completely understand their position among the ancient Celts. On the one hand, they were teachers, ritual leaders and scholars, keeping secret lore. This side is widely recognized in modern writings on the organization. However, the other side of the coin is that the Druids were the diplomats, arbiters and judges of their society, helping to keep the often precarious balance of power and peace between rival chiefdoms and factions in what must have been a complex political environment across ancient Gaul, Britain and Ireland.

The Druids seem to have served as a balancing force by operating as intermediaries between various chiefdoms, and this is probably what Strabo was discussing when he said the Druids "are entrusted with the decision, not only of the private disputes, but of the public disputes as well", to the point that "they even arbitrated cases of war and made the opponents stop when they were about to line up for battle."[8] This role, along with their position as the trusted keepers of wisdom, history and lore, likely ensured that the Druids probably served as a pan-Celtic unifying force in an ever-shifting political landscape.

The Druids were not rewarded these momentous responsibilities with no rhyme or reason. It was not uncommon for a Druid to spend up to two decades in training, studiously familiarizing themselves not only with the lore of their local divine pantheons, but the fields of philosophy, astronomy, ancient verse, and other natural sciences. The Druids, in short, were invested in the concept of reincarnation, meaning that all everlasting souls emerge from their vessels and into another at the time of death. This belief was presumably the basis of their rationalization for human sacrifice, which was performed to relieve or ease the pain of an ailing civilian, and during wartime.

Archaeologists believe that the Druids of Montmartre conducted their sacrifices right on its hilltop, where the Sacré-Cœur would one day rise. At times, several civilians would be thrown into enormous wicker statues carved into the shape of a man, which was then set ablaze. The haunting cries of the condemned, crammed into the cage-like structure of the statue's body, swelled as the roaring flames climbed with frightening efficiency, producing billowing clouds of smoke and ash along with the stench of burning corpses.

A Hallowed Hilltop

A Gallo-Roman temple dedicated either to Mercury or Mars was eventually installed on Montmartre, and according to certain manuscripts dating from the 8th century CE, the locals from centuries past referred to the hill as "Mons Mercori," or "Mount Mercury," consecrated for the Roman god of travelers, merchants, commerce, and the arts. In 9th century texts, on the other

---

8   *The Geography Book IV, Chapter 4:4* by Strabo accessed online at:
    http://penelope.uchicago.edu/Thayer/E/Roman/Texts/Strabo/4D*.html#4.4

hand, the hilltop is cited as "Mons Martis," or "Mars' Mount," suggesting that it was dedicated to the god of war and agriculture.

Whether the Christians began to multiply in Montmartre before or after the construction of these pagan temples remains a matter of dispute. Most historians today lean towards the latter based on the construction date of the hilltop's first Christian chapel, which was built in honor of Saint Denis, the first bishop of Paris, in 270 CE.   As recounted by Hilduin, a 9th century Parisian bishop, Carolingian hagiographer, and abbot of the Saint Denis monastery in the *Miracles of Saint Denis,* Denis was one of seven Italian bishops dispatched to Gaul and tasked with evangelizing the residents of Mons Martis, then suffering under the tyranny of the pagan Roman Emperor Trajan Decius. In the spring of 249 CE (in other accounts, the following year), the emperor issued an edict that ordered all civilians, Christians included, to present sacrificial offerings and tributes to the Roman gods on the hilltop temple on behalf of their beloved emperor. To ensure that all civilians complied, they were made to partake in these pagan rites in the presence of a licensed Roman magistrate and acquire from them a notarized document attesting to their participation. Those who disobeyed the decree were viciously tortured and brutally executed, for their lack of compliance was not only a slight against the gods, but the emperor himself.

Like other Christian martyrs, the hopelessly devout Denis would not bow down to the armor and galea sporting god, nor would he do so for any of the other Roman gods. His refusal to cease his Christian gospel-spreading operations in the locality, as well as accusations of evil sorcery, only added fuel to the flames, and in the autumn of 250 CE (in other accounts, 258 or 270 CE), the brave bishop was arrested and sentenced to death. Under the instructions of a prefect named Fescennius Sisinius, Denis and two of his companions were forcibly undressed and subjected to multiple lashings until blood gushed out of the welts on their raw flesh. Next, the bishop and his doomed disciples were tethered to iron grills overnight, left vulnerable to wild predators, then cooked in a furnace and crucified on separate crosses the following day. Incredibly, Denis and his companions survived these impossible trials with nothing but prayer. The badly-battered men were then whisked back into their prison cells by their baffled guards shortly thereafter, during which time Denis was visited by an apparition of Christ accompanied by a retinue of singing angels, thus marking the first known vision of Christ on the Sacréd hill.

The bishop and his comrades were made to face the blade of execution on the third day of their captivity. After another round of lashings for good measure, the trio was marched to the top of Mons Martis and beheaded by their executioners. To the horror and astonishment of the spectators, the headless body of Denis picked up his head and, initially staggering, walked for about six miles to what would become the city of Saint-Denis, the mouth of his detached head delivering a passionate sermon along the way. Only after completing his sermon did the detached head fall silent and the headless corpse crumple to the ground.

Roughly 20 years following the death of St. Denis, the aforementioned Christian chapel was constructed on the hilltop. It was then that the Mons Martis was rebranded the "Mont des Martyrs," later shortened to its present "Montmartre," in memory of Denis, his companions, and the other unnamed Christian martyrs murdered on the hilltop. Another church devoted to St. Denis – formerly the Saint Denys-la-Chapelle and now the Basilique Royale de Saint-Denis – was constructed on the spot where the martyr dropped dead, a project led by St. Genevieve in 475 CE.

The original hilltop chapel was eventually deserted for reasons unknown and had begun to decay by the 9th century, but local authorities managed to salvage its rotting remains and rebuilt the church anew. The hilltop church was thus revived as a popular pilgrimage site, visited by those en route to the nearby Saint Denys-la-Chapelle. Excavations in recent years show that a number of Christians were fortunate enough to secure a burial spot on the Sacréd hill itself; their bones were collected and placed in a sectioned-off area of the hillside quarry now known as the Martyrium.

A 17th century depiction of the Chapel of the Martyrs

The hilltop chapel was abandoned once more around the 12th century or 13th century, and this time, there would be no major activity there for the next 500 years. Nonetheless, even as the ruins of the hilltop church were eventually removed, the barren hilltop of Montmartre remained to the locals an inviolable place of prayer and miracles. Pilgrims, clergymen, royals, and martyrs in-the-making alike, among them Joan of Arc, St. Bernard, and the fabled St. Germain, continued to hike up to the hill's summit, where they paid homage to Christ and the martyrs, pleaded for solutions to their maladies, and thanked the heavens for auspicious events and other milestones.

One of France's 14th century monarchs, King Charles VI, was one such pilgrim. To say that the sovereign was ill-fated would be an understatement - ever since he was a child, the future king was a magnet for disease and disaster. His multiple delusions, which included his belief that he was glass and therefore literally fragile, as well as the inexplicable illnesses he was afflicted with (including one that prompted all his hair and nails to wither away), only added to the unimaginable weight of his daily burdens. However, on January 28, 1393, the normally disaster-prone monarch was spared by an unlikely stroke of luck. As the story goes, King Charles VI was performing a choreographed jig with other nobles during the *Bal des Ardents* when a fire suddenly erupted. Four of the dancers were killed on the spot, but the king, much to his relief, narrowly escaped the inferno. A few days later, the ailing king limped up to the Martyrium, and later the Montmartre pinnacle, and thanked the Lord profusely for saving his life.

A contemporary depiction of King Charles VI of France

Unfortunately, the reasons for pilgrimages were typically far grimmer. In 1407, war was waged between two competitive branches of male heirs within the French royal family, a 28-year conflict now remembered as the Armagnac-Burgundian Civil War. The continuously spiking death toll of military and civilian casualties galvanized hundreds of members of the Parisian parishes to partake in a solemn procession that culminated at the Montmartre peak, where they formed a seemingly endless chain of linked hands and prayed to St. Denis for the salvation of the city. When King Francois I was wounded, captured, and imprisoned at the Battle of Pavia in 1525, Parisians joined the locals again in another pilgrimage to Montmartre, where they called upon Christ to keep their precious king in His bosom.

The heavens appeared to take no notice of the hilltop's vacancy until the final years of the 17th century, when Christ appeared to a nun at the Montmartre Abbey, Sister Marguerite-Marie Alacoque, in a series of apparitions. This bride of Christ and the clairvoyant Sister Margaret Mary Alacoque, who popularized the Catholic sect known as the "Sacréd Heart of Jesus," the denomination of the Sacré-Cœur, were one and the same.

The Burgundy-born Alacoque, as her biographers claim, seemed to have been blessed from birth. She was a serious, naturally prayerful child, one who preferred to meditate and converse with God in utter silence over gallivanting outdoors with the other neighborhood children. She was so pious, in fact, that she began to subject herself to acute acts of corporal mortification at the age of nine, which, in turn, were so ghastly that she was rendered bedridden until the age of 13. The day before her "instantaneous recovery," a desperate Alacoque vowed to dedicate the rest of her life to her religion in exchange for her health. She incorporated the Virgin Mother's name into hers as a way to solidify her devotion to the pact.

Most of Alacoque's hagiographers believe her encounters with Christ, which began shortly after her 17th birthday, were what spurred her to enter the Visitation Convent at Paray-le-Monial at age 24. It was in this very convent, they say, that Christ fed to her the doctrines of the Sacréd Heart and instructed her to encircle a number of important dates on her calendar. "Eucharistic Adoration," for example, was to be practiced on the so-called "Holy Hour" of each Thursday. Holy Communion was to be distributed only on the first Friday of the month.

Alacoque's first encounter with Christ as a nun at the Visitation Convent came on December 27, 1673, the feast of Saint John, and it is considered the most meaningful of all their interactions. That evening, Christ bestowed upon her a mission in which she was instructed to spread "the flame of the fire of his divine heart" to all of mankind. In the same breath, He imparted to her the basic logistics of the new devotion: the local parish was to hold a special feast of the Sacréd Heart on the Friday after the Corpus Christi; the feast day of the Sacréd Heart itself would be celebrated 19 days after the Pentecost; and the tradition of the Nine First Fridays. Shortly thereafter, Christ appeared to her again, this time urging her to construct a church entirely devoted to the Sacréd Heart of Jesus on the Montmartre hilltop.

Alas, the plans of a new hilltop church were never seriously entertained, at least not in Alacoque's lifetime. Instead, it would take yet another tragedy of even greater proportions for the city's residents to finally follow through on the instructions communicated to them by Christ via Alacoque.

A Vow

The catastrophe that would strike the French towards the latter half of the 19th century was twofold, with the second component being a byproduct of the first. The first was the Armistice of Versailles, which came into effect on January 28, 1871. The ceasefire not only effectively spelled the end of the Franco-Prussian War, it marked the embarrassing surrender and defeat of France, which was grievously injured by the four-month Prussian siege on the capital city. Just days after France's surrender, an affluent pair of brothers-in-law, Alexandre Felix Legentil and Hubert Rohault de Fleury, drafted the National Vow, which called for the construction of what is now the Sacré-Cœur Basilica.

Legentil

A portrait of de Fleury

Legentil was known locally as an enterprising entrepreneur who founded the *Au Petit Saint-Thomas,* then a thriving department store that offered a fresh selection of quality products at low prices, mail order service, and regular sales. The pious Christian man was also adored for his modesty and philanthropy. He attended Church regularly, dressed in homespun outfits, and ate simply, saving his sizable fortune instead for the destitute. In addition to his routine donations to local charities, Legentil organized a successful fundraiser that allowed him to purchase a hefty plot of land in 1856, upon which he built schoolhouses, conference halls, small chapels, and accompanying refectories, many of which still stand today near the Saint-Vincent-de-Paul Church.

Legentil was particularly shaken by the news of the Armistice of Versailles, for he himself was made to live as a refugee in Poitiers when his neighborhood was seized by the Prussians the previous year. Legentil was a disciple of Frederic Ozanam, a scholar, equal rights activist, and founder of the Society of St. Vincent de Paul, which caused more controversy. Legentil was among the "useless mouths" rounded up by the governor and sent into exile just a few days after the fact. Rather than argue for his right to stay, Legentil donated the bulk of his belongings to the needy and headed for Poitiers, where he supposedly put pen to paper and created the National Vow. Having experienced and witnessed the ugliness of war and the sinking morale of his fellow countrymen firsthand, he feared – rightfully so – what was to come, and he hoped that the building of a basilica, a token of the nation's redress, would be enough to secure the Lord's protection of France.

Today, many who are modestly acquainted with the basilica's history erroneously believe that the National Vow – and thus, the concept of the Sacré-Cœur Basilica – was conceived by Legentil and de Fleury, but this was not the case. Towards the end of November 1870, Adolphe Baudon de Mony, the president of the Society of St. Vincent de Paul, received a letter from Monseigneur Beluze, a member of the society's general council. Christians in Lyon, wrote Beluze, had composed a document similar to the contents of the National Vow, and it would be wise for the people of Paris to draw one up themselves. Not only did Baudon de Mony make immediate preparations for a vow to be drafted, he took the initiative to announce to Louis Veuillot, editor of the Catholic, radically pro-papacy newspaper *L'Univers,* his plans for a construction of a church on the Montmartre summit. Veuillot reported on these plans in his paper at once, a story that ran as early as December 13, 1870.

Baudon de Mony

Veuillot

    Meanwhile, Baudon de Mony had selected Legentil, one of his most trusted society subordinates, as the author of the National Vow. Legentil was thrilled to have been entrusted with such an honorable task, but when he learned of Baudon de Mony's intentions to dedicate the potential basilica to the Virgin Mary, he argued that they break away from the norm and customize the sanctuary for the cult of the Sacréd Heart and Sister Alacoque's teachings instead. Baudon de Mony and the society's general council were understandably hesitant about Legentil's stipulation, and in response, cited the cult's still-incipient status and the resulting difficulty in obtaining the funds needed for a project of this size. The matter remained in limbo, at least for the time being.

    Shortly after putting down his copy of *Le Triomphe de la France par le Couer de Jesus ("The Triumph of France through the Heart of Jesus")* on December 8, 1870, Legentil wrote a letter to the booklet's author, Father Boylesve, and recounted to him his exchanges with Baudon de Mony:

"Reverend Father,

Some days ago, I received a letter from Mr. Baudon...in which the following passage drew my attention:

'Mr. Beluze (founder of the Catholic Circle of Luxembourg), in announcing to me that the city of Lyon had vowed to rebuild Notre-Dame de Fourviere, in the event that the town be spared, proposed that a similar vow be made in Paris. What do you think? It would be a fine but difficult gesture. However, there is a need for churches to be built in the neighboring areas and *Notre-Dame de la Delivrance* would be an appropriate name, if we obtain this deliverance.' I replied immediately to...Baudon that I was favorable to this idea and that I would subscribe to the construction of such a church...or to a church dedicated to the Sacréd Heart."

Legentil continued, lamenting on the stalemate of their discussions: "Baudon insists on a vow to build a church in Paris, to be called...the Notre-Dame de la Delivrance, and he rightly notes that it would be useful to create a parish in an area where churches are lacking, in order to obtain the indispensable support of the Archbishop...On the advice of my good friend Mr. Bain, I am writing to...seek your advice and support in spreading the idea I have just outlined and that I do not presume to have invented. You shall see through what means it is possible to obtain subscriptions among those exiled from Paris that you can reach in Le Mans, Poitiers, and elsewhere, as well as people around the country, because at the moment, the cause of Paris is the cause of France."

When the deadlock of the basilica's denomination persisted, Legentil, who had promised to Father Gustave Argand, the rector of the Jesuit College of Saint Joseph de Poitiers, to fully commit himself to the endeavor, took matters into his own hands. In the early months of February 1871, Legentil completed the first draft of the Vow to the Sacréd Heart, alternatively known as the "Vow of Poitiers" and later rebranded as the National Vow. Legentil presented stacks of the vow, which pleaded to the heavens for the deliverance and protection of the capital city, to Louis Edouard Pie, the Bishop of Poitiers, and sought from him his public endorsement and permission to distribute the pamphlets. Bishop Pie agreed to publish the vow in the Poitiers diocesan bulletin and allowed Legentil to hand out the pamphlets as he so pleased, but the bishop refused to promote the project any further. Even so, Legentil took the bishop's distance from the vow in stride and sought the help of his brother-in-law de Fleury, a former navy apprentice officer who had since become an artist. Together, they circulated printed copies of the vow across France and even some areas in Switzerland.

The first draft of the Vow reads, "In the presence of the misfortunes that have befallen France and the greater misfortunes that perhaps still threaten her. In the presence of the sacrilegious attacks committed in Rome against the rights of the Church and the Holy See and against the Sacréd person of the Vicar of Jesus Christ. We humble ourselves before God and uniting in our love both Church and Fatherland, recognize that we have sinned and been justly punished...And to make honorable amends for our sins and obtain through the infinite mercy of the Sacréd Heart of Our Lord Jesus Christ pardon for our faults, as well as the extraordinary help that alone can...put an end to the misfortunes of France, we hereby promise to contribute to the construction, in Paris, of a sanctuary dedicated to the Sacréd Heart of Jesus (the Sacré-Cœur)."

The chief purpose of the Sacré-Cœur was to demonstrate the nation's remorse for its corruption and wickedness, as well as remorse over the 40,000 souls lost during the French Revolution and the 58,000 killed in the Franco-Prussian War. Legentil, on behalf of the Parisians, pledged to raise funds for the construction of a hilltop basilica in the hopes that France would be protected from further harm. At the same time, it was hoped that the presence of a striking and praiseworthy structure would uplift the spirits of the forlorn Parisians.

However, further distribution of the National Vow and the campaign for the basilica's construction came to a halt just a few weeks after it began, for unbeknownst to Legentil and de Fleury, the Paris Commune was swiftly taking shape, which cost the lives of tens of thousands more civilians. The French were, at this stage, comprised of mostly the working class, with as many as 500,000 earning their bread and butter as industrial laborers alone. For decades, the disgruntled laborers protested against government-sanctioned injustices, among them the lopsided taxation system. They voiced their anxieties regarding the disproportionate distribution of wealth and expressed their discontent with the corruption that was rife within the rigged system, yet time and time again, their objections fell on deaf ears. By the humiliating end of the Franco-Prussian War, which took a toll on the already bleeding finances of many, the working class decided they would be silenced no longer.

The Third Republic, which prepared to take the reins following the signing of the armistice, was suspiciously abundant in royalists. Fearing the revival of monarchism and feeling betrayed by what they deemed the cowardice of the armistice signers, 2 million Parisians, a majority of whom were workers and students, rallied behind the Commune, a democratically elected socialist government that promoted policies shaped by Marxist and First International ideals. It was, as described by some historians, the "first truly democratic government in all of France," a government operated by "radicals" who led "the first working-class revolt." The Commune was backed by members of the National Guard, which staved off the French army and grappled for command of the city's government buildings and munitions. The National Guard succeeded in securing the government buildings and munitions on March 18, 1871, marking the start of the Commune's rule.

The Commune remained in power for about two months, and though it was always controversial, it was founded with good intentions. The autonomous council, or "Communards," as they called themselves, consisted of 60 members, all of whom held equal power. They were from all walks of life, including laborers, businessmen, scholars, journalists, and so on. From the start, the Communards retired the law of compulsory enlistment, discontinued the death penalty, and declared the separation of church and state, which meant that religion was no longer a required component of school curricula. In the same vein, church-owned estates became public property. The council also issued socialist policies that evened out the playing field for all classes across the board, reversing several privileges that unfairly oppressed those in the lower echelons.

To the dismay of the Commune's adherents, its existence was short-lived, largely due to incessant assaults by the French army. On May 21, 1871, the army descended upon Paris, massacred 20,000 Parisians, and replanted the flag of the Third Republic. 750 soldiers were killed in the melee as the Communards and the National Guard assembled makeshift barricades and did their best to fend off the soldiers, but their efforts were to no avail. They were left with no choice but to raise the white flag just one week later, signaling the dissolution of the Commune.

At the end of the entire affair, just about everyone's hands were stained with blood. On May 24, Communard Théophile Ferré ordered the execution of six high-profile prisoners, including Archbishop of Paris Georges Darboy. Following the surrender of the Communards, another 38,000 were taken hostage, and more than 7,000 were deported by the army under orders from the Third Republic. Those who were forcibly relocated were ultimately given the longer end of the stick, for many of those imprisoned were mercilessly put to death in a rampage now referred to as Semaine Sanglante ("Bloody Week"). Ferré himself was ultimately executed.

Ferré

Needless to say, Paris was a living hell and redemption was needed more than ever. On January 18, 1872, Darboy's successor, Archbishop Joseph-Hippolyte Guibert, approved Legentil's revised Vow to the Sacréd Heart. The redrafted document, as prescribed by the decree of the Assemblee Nationale, now included its intentions to "expiate the crimes of the [Paris] Commune," and reiterated its choice of the Montmartre crest as the site of the new basilica.

Archbishop Guibert

Interestingly enough, Archbishop Guibert was apparently beset by second thoughts in the months following his public advocacy of the Vow of Poitiers. Whatever reservations he had with the pledge, however, melted away in mid-October 1872, when he trekked up the Montmartre Hill to appraise the site of the would-be basilica for himself. It was on the summit of the Montmartre, as he stood upon a patch of sun-soaked grass and breathed in the morning mist, that he was reportedly struck by a vision. The cotton-like clouds above him parted like curtains, allowing a golden river of sunlight to flow through, but it was the thunderous, but soothing voice in the sky that stopped him in his tracks. The voice boomed, "It is here. It is here where the martyrs are, and as such, it is here that the Sacréd Heart must reign so that it can beckon all to come."

Building Hope

"In him we have redemption through his blood, the forgiveness of our trespasses, according to the riches of his grace." – Ephesians 1:7

On July 24, 1873, Legentil and Archbishop Guibert rejoiced as the National Assembly instituted a law that effectively declared the Sacré-Cœur a private property of public interest that would shield it from attempts at intervention, or so they thought. The law was essentially the permit needed to begin construction on the Montmartre peak. Furthermore, the Works Committee of 1872, along with Parliament the following year, voted to rechristen the Vow to the Sacréd Heart as the "National Vow." This meant it was no longer an undertaking exclusive to Parisians, but a cause to be embraced by the entire country.

As predicted, the decision to dedicate the basilica to the Sacréd Heart cult was greeted by a number of raised eyebrows. The Sacré-Cœur was not the only establishment under way - there was the Notre-Dame de Garde in Marseilles and the Notre-Dame de Fourviere in Lyon, to name a few - but all these basilicas were designed for the Blessed Mother (the Marian cult being the most prevalent in France at the time). These light whispers of disfavor would only heighten with time.

Originally, the founders of the Sacré-Cœur hoped to share the brunt of the bills with a collection of other rich benefactors. Once it was determined a public project, they opened up funding to the French masses, allowing pilgrims and even non-Christian civilians, whether matter rich or poor, to pitch in. The names of many of these donors were later etched into the walls of the basilica to eternally memorialize their contributions.

Bishop Pie, who was previously reluctant to exhibit his espousal of the cause, now voiced it uninhibitedly. He addressed his congregation with the same spirited opener he used for most of his sermons, but they were now packed with new meaning. He encouraged, albeit indirectly, his flock to receive the new basilica at Montmartre with open arms, or at the very least an open mind. He told his listeners, "The hour of the Church is upon us…The hour approaches when Jesus Christ will return not only to the hearts and minds of men, but also to the institutions, the social life, and the public life of the peoples."

On February 1, 1874, the men behind the Sacré-Cœur's launched a competition that called upon the nation's best architects to conjure up an original design for the basilica. A total of 78 architects pounced upon the offer and scrambled for the honor. The pool was eventually narrowed down to a dozen finalists, and the winner, a seasoned architectural maven by the name of Paul Abadie, was chosen on the 30th of June. The 62-year-old Abadie, a native Parisian, was the son of nationally established veteran architect Paul Abadie, Sr. Abadie, Sr., who carved his name into the industry with his distinctively Neo-Classical style, was the mastermind behind the timeless *Palais de Justice* in Angouleme and the aesthetically kindred *Saint-Jacques de l'Houmeau* church. The monotone cream and beige color scheme and the Neo-Romanesque pillars seen in Abadie, Sr.'s works were later adopted by his son and woven into many of his own designs, including the Sacré-Cœur.

Abadie

The thought of living up to Abadie, Sr.'s name without appearing to have hitched a ride on his coattails was challenging to say the least, but Abadie was resolved to give it a try. To begin with, he enrolled at and received a diploma from the *Ecole des Beaux-Arts*, the most reputable Fine Arts academy in the capital.

While Abadie is now most renowned for his involvement in the Sacré-Cœur, he was not merely a designer. In fact, he started out in the field of structural restoration. He was appointed *attache* (an ambassador-appointed specialist) by the *Commision des Monuments Historiques* (The Commission for Historical Monuments) and embarked on an educational and hands-on tour of medieval architecture sponsored by that commission. The tour presumably sparked Abadie's interest in the restoration of medieval buildings and landmarks. Rather than compete with his father, Abadie chose to partner with him, hiring Abadie, Sr. as an inspector for diocesan buildings situated in Angouleme in 1849. Simultaneously, the ambitious son continued to flesh out his own portfolio. He earned himself the title of designer and senior architect for a few buildings, including the town hall, the churches of Chatou and Saint Georges of Mussidan, and Mailleberchie Castle in Villebois-Lavalette. He invested the better part of his time, however, on the restoration of national monuments, such as Notre-Dame, the Eglise Sainte-Croix in Bordeaux, and the St. Front Cathedral in Perigeux, proceeding to breathe new life into more than 40 churches in his lifetime.

Abadie's efforts were duly rewarded when he was named General Inspector of Diocesan Buildings in 1872. In July 1874, about a month after the selection of his design, Abadie was appointed the official Diocesan Architect for Paris.

Abadie was thoroughly aware of the magnitude of the responsibility thrust upon him, and he was determined not to disappoint. His interpretation of the nation's penance would have to be subtly and delicately elegant so as to reflect the somberness of their intentions, but splendid and memorable enough to satisfy the basilica's supporters, critics, and subjects. He trusted his instincts and dug deep into his roots, relying on what he knew best, but at the same time, he dared to think outside of the box and tie the design together with his own unique twist.

Ultimately, Abadie settled upon a sleek facade with a predominantly white theme symbolizing purity and forgiveness, sprinkled with elements borrowed from a variety of sources. The Roman-Byzantine flavor of the Sacré-Cœur paid homage to certain classics he helped restore, such as the St. Front Cathedral, an austere, handsome grayscale structure notably featuring stout, circular domes crowned by conical spires with cross ornaments. He also looked to outside sources, including Venice's St. Mark's Basilica, a pearl-colored monument with plump, perfectly round cupolas garnished with bulb-shaped spires. Abadie even found inspiration in the Hagia Sofia in Istanbul, paying special attention to the exquisite masonry and the Romanesque colonnades and arch-work in its interior.

As a result, the Sacré-Cœur, as a whole, was a complete departure from the medieval, Gothic-style architecture adopted by the rest of the city's churches. As such, it eschewed Gothic characteristics such as flamboyance, overindulgence in symmetry, geometric shapes and patterns, and the hard, clear-cut lines and precision in silhouettes.

The foundation stone of the Sacré-Cœur was installed on June 16, 1875, and while it was obviously a memorable event, the enthusiasm behind it was almost immediately stooped in itrs tracks by the first of many roadblocks. These obstacles ranged from small, easily resolvable snags to full-blown conundrums.

Not long after the ceremonial planting of the foundation stone, Abadie's team reported back to him with a pressing issue: there were quarries located directly underneath the Montmartre crest, which meant that the strength of the earth alone was not enough to shore up a church of such a size.

After some deliberation, Abadie's team executed what they believed to be the soundest solution. They drilled a hole in the earth with a depth of roughly 108.2 feet (33 meters) until the laborers touched hard rock, and then they filled the yawning crater with 83 supportive stone pillars that aimed to strengthen the basilica's foundations. The editors of the *Basilique du Sacré-Cœur de Montmartre*, the basilica's official website, summed up the problem: "Without these pillars, the [Sacré-Cœur] would have sunk into the soil."

Much to the chagrin of the basilica's founders, they would soon be plagued with problems that weren't quite as simple to rectify. The logistical setbacks and intractable political issues were so exhausting that it ultimately took the Sacré-Cœur more than four decades to complete.

In 1878, Abadie authorized his team to apply the final touches to the blueprints for the basilica's crypt, but construction was continuously stalled by the resistance of those who strongly opposed the symbolism of the Sacré-Cœur. In 1880, members of the *Conseil Municipal* participated in a succession of debates concerning the basilica. Critics of the Sacré-Cœur were nothing new, but it was during these dialogues that the specific complaints of the opposing parties were aired on a concentrated public platform for the first time. Former Communards, for example, labeled the initiators and blind patrons of the Sacré-Cœur as monarchist sympathizers and primitive traditionalists. In their eyes, the basilica's supporters were hypocrites who claimed to be honoring the lives lost as a consequence of France's wars, but in actuality they were harboring their own rightist agendas. According to the ex-Communards, supporters of the basilica wanted France to revert to the archaic monarchical period, which they blasted as "a slap in the face of reason."

The Sacré-Cœur was also targeted by the partisans of the Third Republic. Republican statesman Leon Gambetta called the project "an incessant provocation to civil war." Many in this camp actively campaigned to repeal the 1873 law that privatized the basilica, for lack of a better term, but their efforts were all for naught. Thus, the Republicans poured their efforts into unwrapping the problematic nature of the basilica's symbolism instead, and, in direct contrast to the basilica's ex-Communard opponents, they accused the Sacré-Cœur of being its founders' secret salute to the Commune. The Montmartre hilltop's legacy as a center for martyrs and a place of solace for pious pilgrims, the Republicans asserted, was incontrovertibly marred by the Commune. The basilica, they were quick to point out, was built atop the very spot where French Generals Jacques Leon-Clement-Thomas and Claude Lecomte were ambushed and captured by the National Guard, considered by most chroniclers the event that set off the formation of the Commune. As such, they savaged the Sacré-Cœur's founders for tastelessly selecting the setting of the Commune's first rebellion as the site of their basilica and disrespecting the memories of these generals, who were later mowed down by the guns of the National Guard (Lecomte was found with nine "balls" pierced into his back, and Clement-Thomas suffered 40).

The Republicans also questioned how the initiators managed to score such potent support from the Church. Some singled out Archbishop Guibert himself, whose predecessor, along with 24 other innocent clergymen, were slaughtered by the revolutionaries following the collapse of the Commune.

In response, supporters of the Sacré-Cœur contended that this was all the more reason to raise a house of God in this very location. Not only would the Sacré-Cœur serve as penance for the atrocities committed by all sides, it would help to restore the sanctity of Montmartre.

The construction crew of the Sacré-Cœur did its utmost to rise above the hate, but workers could accomplish little even on a good day, for the tide of protests steadily swelled for over a decade. In Emile Zola's famous work *Paris*, Guillaume Froment is infamous for his unambiguous hatred of the Sacré-Cœur, as evidenced by his bid to rig the basilica with explosives and blast it into the air. In one passage, Froment declared, "I know of no more idiotic nonsense, Paris crowned, dominated by this idolatrous temple (the Sacré-Cœur), built to glorify the absurd." In another part of the book, Froment disdainfully referred to the structure as the "Basilica of the Ridiculous." Similarly, the Sacré-Cœur was poetically dismissed as a "lunatic's confectionery dream" by another unnamed Parisian.

Due to the Sacré-Cœur's seeming unpopularity, delays remained constant. When Abadie died in 1884, only the foundations of the basilica and a rough impression of the crypt had been cast. The construction crew would only begin to dive into the project in full during the spring of 1881, approximately six years after the installation of the foundation stone.

A March 1882 picture of the basilica's construction

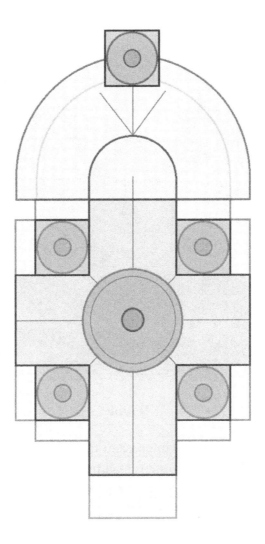

The plan for the basilica's roofs

Abadie's shoes were filled by another experienced architect, Honore Daumet, a fellow alumni of the Academy of Fine Arts and a previous winner of the *Grand Prix de Rome,* one of the most prestigious awards for French art students. He, too, was the bearer of a glittering portfolio, which included the western facade of the Palace of Justice and the restoration of the Chapel of the Palace of Versailles. Daumet's tenure as chief architect may have been shorter than that of his forerunner, but it was certainly more productive.

Daumet

The captivating, almost lustrous ivory-whiteness of the basilica's exterior – later made accessible by a straight flight of about 300 steps leading up to the pinnacle of the Montmartre – is easily one of the site's most extraordinary features. Although the basilica's construction began nearly 150 years ago, the all-white facade remains seemingly unblemished, looking almost new. The agelessness of the basilica is courtesy of its travertine stone building blocks, firm, resilient, high-quality material sought after for their durability and "self-cleaning" properties.

The white limestone, otherwise known as the "Chateau-Landon," was sourced from the quarries in the Souppes-sur-Loing, a commune in the Seine-et-Marne department in north-central France. The same type of travertine stone was used in the construction of the Alexandre III Bridge in Paris, the Arc de Triomphe, and the tiling in the Pantheon. Travertine, also classed as granite, is known to discharge calcite when met with rainwater. It is a white, grainy mineral brimming with calcium carbonate, which naturally bleached its surface, allowing the stone to retain its pristine quality. In addition, the travertine was dazzlingly radiant when set against the inky black canvas of the night, and when that canvas was dotted with twinkling stars, the splendid structure looked like the most dazzling diamond in the sky. Though the stars are now constantly shrouded by pollution, the Sacré-Cœur remains a magnificent sight, an impenetrable pillar of white peeking out from the haze.

Luis Sanchez's picture of the exterior

The basilica at night

Next, Daumet started work on the basilica's domed cupolas, which gave the Sacré-Cœur its iconic silhouette. The roof of the central dome, which hovers about 272.3 feet (83 meters) off the ground, was propped up by nearly 80 pillars, each column capped with ornate Corinthian-inspired capitals. The dome was slimmer and more egg-shaped, so it is not quite as spherical as the domes of the Venetian St. Mark's Basilica or the Taj Mahal. It was coated with neat rows of blocks shaped like mitres or miniature stock shields, punctuated by decorative borders. A semi-teardrop-shaped roof was snugly fitted over the small colonnade that surmounted the dome. This smaller roof also had a texture reminiscent of fish scales and was ornamented with a cross perched atop its crown, as seen in the St. Front Cathedral.

The doughnut-shaped gallery within the dome was eventually opened to the masses, accessible only by a spiral staircase. Visitors soon found the climb was well worth it, for they were treated to a panoramic view of Paris, including the neighboring city of Saint Denis, the Pantheon, the Eiffel Tower, and the Montparnasse Tower, among other landmarks. The basilica's smaller domes, roughly 180.5 feet (55 meters) tall with a diameter of 52.5 feet (16 meters), were replicas of the central dome.

The first of the three statues posted at the main entrance of the basilica, which served as its guardians, was installed around this time. Hovering over the entrance in a large, arch-shaped niche is a statue of Christ, about 16.5 feet (5 meters) in height and depicted with a beard and shoulder-length curls. Christ's right hand was raised with the ring finger and little fingers furled, blessing those before Him. Under the niche was the Latin inscription "Cor Jesu Sacratissimum," which translates into "The Most Sacréd Heart of Jesus."

Like Abadie, Daumet strove to disregard the basilica's critics, but progress continued to be impeded by the still-growing enmity towards the Sacré-Cœur. Elizabeth Emery, author of *Romancing the Cathedral: Gothic Architecture in Fin-de-Siecle French Culture,* described some of the criticism directed at the basilica: "[I]n the Third Republic, the Sacré-Cœur...was a symbol of antiquated oppression. Not only were the values on which it was constructed – God and king – antithetical to the Republic, but even its shape recalled Victor Hugo's theories about the relationship between form and historical trend...[Hugo] had written that domes represented the oppression of theocracy, while arches revealed the liberty of democracy...To Republicans, the domed capital of the Sacré-Cœur evoked Saint Peter's of Rome, thus incarnating the political domination of the Vatican. The basilica's position, looming over the Pantheon, the Republican temple of reason, added insult to injury, especially when the basilica's fundraisers insisted on the basilica's grandeur...Such antagonism caused Republican leaders...to target clericalism as the enemy of the French people...The Sacré-Cœur [was] a visual reminder of the Republic's enemy, the Catholic Church..."

Ultimately, try as they might, the Sacré-Cœur's opponents could do little more than inconvenience its builders with temporary hindrances. The 1873 law rendered the basilica virtually untouchable, and the Sacré-Cœur was financed by private donations, so the basilica lay outside of the government's jurisdiction.

On August 1, 1885, Archbishop Guibert conducted the official ceremony for the Perpetual Adoration of the Eucharist. The modest congregation gathered at what would become the 200-foot-long nave of the church with the dome above it only partially finished, and the archbishop performed the sacrament on the basilica's grounds for the first time. Upon entering, the bulging eyes of the visitors were immediately drawn to the High Altar, a glinting bronze shrine that would one day be set against a medley of white marble statues of Christ on a crucifix flanked by the 12 Disciples. The ceiling above the unfinished ceiling, which would one day house its most famous mosaic, would have been barren, and the nave was barely furnished, but the worshipers were unbothered by the underwhelming aesthetics. The gilded ciborium, the receptacle used to hold the body of Christ, was later locked away in a temporary tabernacle placed just behind the altar.

The nave of the Sacré-Cœur has been buzzing with activity ever since. The humble congregation experienced consistent growth over time, seeing a flush of new faces following its eventual completion. Every single day, for all 365 days of the year, men, women, and children milled in and out of the basilica, each offering personal prayers, sincere invocations, and silent devotions of adoration for the Sacré-Cœur. When asked about the purpose of these prayers,

Father Jean Laverton, the current rector of the Sacré-Cœur, answered, "From the top of the [Sacré-Cœur], when the doors are open on the great city of Paris, the Sacréd Body of Christ, given up in this love than which none is greater, is there, displayed and given to all without reserve, offered up to call us to this place where, in the interior dialogue of prayer, He seeks to draw our presence to His presence, to establish His life in us. In the prayer of perpetual adoration, the [whole] world is brought before God by those who pray."

Daumet retired from his post in 1886, and the torch was passed on to architect Jean-Charles Laisné, a native of Studies in the French commune of Fontenay-aux-Roses. His career path followed a similar trajectory to that of Abadie and Daumet, as he was also a graduate of the *Ecole des Beaux-Arts*. Eight years after acquiring his diploma, Laisné, a devotee of Parisian architectural legends Jacques-Marie Huve and Charles Lenormand (famed for their preference of Neoclassical architectural styles), was awarded the Grand Prix of Rome. He was then employed as an architect for the *Commision des Monuments Historiques* and worked alongside other eminent architects to restore priceless historical establishments such as the Narbonne Cathedral and the Pont du Gard. Like Abadie, Laisné was also appointed diocesan architects for the communes of Auch and Gap in southern France.

Laisné presided over the construction of the basilica until 1891, which included resuming work on the facade, the domes, and some of the interior. In that way, he gradually began completing the blueprints passed down by his predecessors.

On November 6, 1887, 14-year-old Therese Martin, now known as St. Therese of Lisieux, journeyed up to the Montmartre crest. Therese was accompanied by her father, the Blessed Louis Martin, her 18-year-old sister Celine, and 194 other pilgrims destined for Rome. The pilgrimage had been coordinated by the Coutances diocese to pay tribute to the 50th anniversary of Pope Leo XIII's ordination.

The three family members, along with the rest of the pilgrimage group, attended Mass at the Sacré-Cœur that Sunday, held in the Chapel of St. Peter, situated inside the basilica's crypt and directly under the apse of the church. Bishop Abel-Anastase Germain, one of the organizers of the pilgrimage, looked down on the unfamiliar faces in his congregation and welcomed them. He announced, "The first station of our great voyage to the tomb of the Apostles will take place in the sanctuary of Montmartre, at this here altar of Saint Peter, erected by the generous gifts of the people of my diocese." Next, Germain retrieved the ciborium and shredded the Eucharist in his hands, reciting to the receivers the motto of the basilica as written in the National Vow: "France pertinent and devoted to the Most Sacréd Heart of Jesus Christ."

Then, young Therese watched with fluttering heart and lips slightly ajar as the bishop took central stage, pacing back and forth as he unleashed his powerful sermon. "We are gathered here in the Chapel of St. Peter," said Germain. "Isn't Peter a model of penitence? You know [it] by how many tears – and what tears! – he cried during his triple denial... Wasn't Peter a model of devotions?...Devotion of knowledge by faith...Don't you hear him say to the Lord: 'You are the Christ, living son of God?'...Devotion of the heart through love...Don't you seem to hear coming from this statue paid for by your pennies this response made by the head of the Apostles to the Savior: 'Oh, yes, Lord, you know that I love you!'"?"

Germain paused for effect before saying, "During our voyage let us all be moved like St. Peter, by the spirit of penitence, the spirit of faith, the spirit of obedience, and above all, by the spirit of love. Oh! Yes, let us love like Peter!... We are on the Martyrs' Hill...Now, who were the martyrs? Their spilled blood cries to us: 'Penitence, devotion, faith, obedience, and love!'"

Therese's soul, they say, was so stirred by the riveting rhetoric of the bishop and the presence of Christ that she decided to officially devote her life to the Sacréd Heart at the altar of Saint Peter. True to her word, Therese joined a cloistered Carmelite convent a year later, at the age of 15. Shortly after she returned home from the pilgrimage, Therese placed her gold bracelet – her most valuable piece of jewelry – into a satin pouch and donated it to the Sacré-Cœur so that it could be liquefied and fused into the gold used for the edges of the basilica's main tabernacle. The thought that her bracelet, which once kissed her skin, would be placed next to the body of her beloved Christ for eternity made her heart soar.

Therese

Therese was not the only pilgrim to declare themselves a servant of Christ in the Crypt of the Sacré-Cœur. On June 6, 1889, the basilica received a former French army officer, ex-refugee of the Franco-Prussian War, and born-again Christian of sorts by the name of Charles de Foucauld. De Foucauld had heard many a story about the wondrous and transformative experiences of those who had previously set foot in the incomplete basilica, but he kept his expectations in check. He wasn't simply a habitual churchgoer - after rediscovering his faith, de Foucauld, determined to live a life mirroring that of Christ by traveling to the Holy Land and living as a hermit in Morocco, Algeria, and Nazareth for a few years.

Although the basilica was far from finished at this point, de Foucauld was taken with the Sacré-Cœur at once, and, before long, he became one of the basilica's most frequent visitors. Not only would de Foucauld pledge to dedicate his life to God and the Sacréd Heart in this crypt, he supposedly stitched the emblem of the Sacréd Heart, – a bleeding (usually punctured by an arrow) heart girdled by a wreath of thorns, crowned by a flaming cross and set inside of a sun, on his hermetic habit. Like Therese, de Foucauld fulfilled his promise just months later when he joined a French chapter of the Cistercian Trappist order. He was ordained in Viviers in 1901, and years later, the basilica honored the hermetic priest by incorporating his image on one of the stained glass windows.

The following is the prayer de Foucauld composed for Christ while at the Sacré-Cœur:

"Most Sacréd Heart of Jesus,

Thank You for revealing Yourself to our eyes, for giving Yourself to us,

For giving us Your infinite presence, in Your Most Holy Eucharist, on the Blessed Altar.

Thank You for giving Yourself, for revealing Yourself, for remaining with us,

All day, all night, at any hour, all our life,

Thus transforming our life into a truly divine life.

Thank You, Most Sacréd Heart of Jesus,

For this excess of goodness, for this excess of happiness."

On June 5, 1891, almost two years after the Sacré-Cœur was first graced with de Foucauld's presence, Cardinal Francois-Marie-Benjamin Richard, who succeeded Guibert, inaugurated the Sacré-Cœur, consecrating it irreversibly for the Solemnity of the Sacréd Heart.

De Foucauld

A Lasting Legacy

"It is your task to be the sentinels of the morning who announce the arrival of the sun, which is the resurrected Christ....The new way of looking at the world and our fellow man, which comes from Him, allows us to penetrate more deeply the mystery of faith, which is an experience to assimilate, a truth to live, the salt and light of reality." – Pope John Paul II

Henri-Pierre-Marie Rauline replaced Laisné as chief architect of the Sacré-Cœur in 1891 and held this title until 1904. Born in the commune of Saint-Pierre-Langers in Normandy, Rauline was yet another graduate of the Academy of Fine Arts. He seemed, at first glance, to be the perfect candidate, for he was a protege of both Abadie and Daumet, working for some time in their workshops at the start of his career. He was also later employed as a subordinate monument inspector by Abadie. Rauline added color to his portfolio with various restoration projects, many of which he was commissioned to work on as the inspector of diocesan buildings, as well as a handful of original designs such as the spire of the belfry in the Church of Saint-Pair de Sartilly.

A local man named Charles Garnier was appointed consulting architect of the Sacré-Cœur and the National Vow Committee, so he collaborated directly with Rauline for the fourth phase of the basilica's construction. Garnier was also an alumni of the *Ecole des Beaux-Arts*, and he was the former apprentice of Neoclassical specialist Louis-Hippolyte Lebas. Garnier was tenured as the professor of architectural history at the Fine Arts Academy, and it did not take long for Garnier to carve out a niche for himself. He was honored with a seat in the architecture department of the *Institut de France*. Garnier, however, is best known for his original work, which included the Opera de Monte-Carlo and the Palais Garnier.

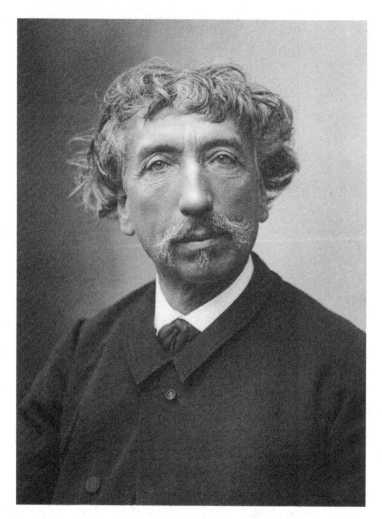

Garnier

The understated Neoclassical sophistication infused in Rauline's work and the baroque elements found in Garnier's were a match made in heaven. All the architects educated at the Fine Arts Academy would have been well-versed in the particular architectural style art historians now call Beaux-Arts. This style was inspired by French Neoclassicism, Gothic architecture, and Renaissance art, but it also incorporated modern construction materials like iron.

Once the basilica's five cupolas were completed, Rauline and Garnier began to lay the foundations for a clock and bell tower. As a gesture of goodwill, the four dioceses of Savoy in the Alps donated to the basilica a gargantuan gift even before the campanile's completion. This gift in question was the *Savoyarde*, which was at one point the largest bell in the world and still remains the fifth largest on the continent. This bell commemorated the country's annexation of Savoy in 1860. The absolute unit weighed over 20 tons and measured about 10 feet (approximately 3 meters) across, to be held up by gudgeons and bearings weighing about 16,270 pounds. The clapper of the behemoth bell weighed a whopping 2,645 pounds.

A postcard featuring the *Savoyarde*

Construction on the *Savoyarde* began on May 13, 1891 in the Annecy workshop of the locally renowned Paccard Brothers, who were among the finest bellmakers in the entire country. There is some confusion as to when the *Savoyarde* was delivered to the basilica - in some accounts, the bell arrived on October 16, 1895, the feast day of Saint Marguerite Marie, and in others, it arrived on November 20 of the same year. Of course, the transportation of the gargantuan bell up the Montmartre was quite literally an uphill struggle. Dozens of men hoisted the *Savoyarde* onto a massive wagon drawn by over 20 horses and maneuvered it around on thick wooden slabs that acted as sleds. In 1969, the *Savoyarde* was joined by four other bells: the Louise, Nicole, Felicite, and Elisabeth, which were rescued from a church that had recently shut down in the commune of Saint-Roch.

The bell was tolled only on the most important religious holidays, such as Christmas, Easter, the Pentecost, the Days of Ascension and Assumption, and All Saints' Day. The crisp, silvery cry of the *Savyoarde's* song, which harmonized beautifully with its accompanying quartet of bells, could be heard from as far as 6 miles away. Sadly, a serpentine crack appeared on the rusted, but otherwise unmarred surface of the *Savoyarde* in the 1990s.

The slender Sacré-Cœur bell tower was only completed by Rauline's successor in 1912. From a fair distance, the difference in the heights of the campanile and the central dome of the basilica seems microscopic, with the former surpassing the latter by just one meter. The belfry was a complementary Roman-Byzantine piece, also equipped with its own gallery. Its roof is more funnel than ovoid-shaped, but it was covered with a similar ribbed surface and was surmounted by an even more petite version of the domes' miniature colonnades.

Between 1900 and 1922, three local artists – Luc-Olivier Merson, Henri-Marcel Magne, and R. Martin – were commissioned to enliven the nude, borderline unsightly apse above the High Altar in the central nave. What resulted was the majestic mosaic mural entitled *Christ in Majesty*, among the largest of its kind in the world. The centerpiece of this stellar masterpiece, which had been painstakingly pieced together for over two decades, was undoubtedly Jesus Christ, portrayed with arms outstretched, a representation of the resurrected Christ, as well as "France's devotion to the Sacréd Heart." The rest of those depicted in the mural were easily dwarfed by Christ, seen clothed in a flowing, lace-white robe. The golden, almost foil-like material used to fill in the glowing heart and the halos of Christ and His companions winked flashes of light.

A picture of the interior

Surrounding Christ in varying sizes and levels were a diverse assemblage of worshipers, of which included prominent ecclesiastical figures and the various patron saints of France and Europe. The figures on the bottom level of the pantheon were divvied up into two groups and were placed on either side of Christ, standing underneath the arches of identical, interlinked domed monuments.

The official website of the *Sacré-Cœur* lists the figures seen to the left of Christ, the so-called "Homage of the Catholic Church," in the following passage: "From the left, Pope Clement XIII who instituted the feast of the Sacréd Heart; Pope Pius IX who extended it to the universal Church; Pope Leo XIII (offering the globe) consecrating the human race to the Sacréd Heart. These are followed by figures symbolizing the five continents."

The following are the names of those depicted to the right of Christ, "For the Homage of France to the Sacréd Heart": "From the right, various historical events linking France to the Sacréd Heart are recalled: the vow of Marseilles during the plague of 1720; the vow of the Temple with Louis XVI and the royal family in 1792; the National Vow of Generals Sonis and de Charette carrying the banner of the Sacréd Heart in 1870; the initiators of the Vow...Legentil and de Fleury in 1871; the reporter on the draft law at the French Parliament (1873); [and finally] the Cardinals of Paris (Archbishops Guibert, Richard, and Amette) who cooperated in the building and embellishment of the [Sacré-Cœur]."

The same article also identifies the saints and martyrs on the second level of the pantheon. Saints typically associated with the Sacréd Heart of Jesus were displayed on the left-hand corner above Christ's shoulders, and the patron saints of France to His right: "[To the left of Christ, the "Heavenly Church"]: Saints Peter, John, Paul, Ignatius of Antioch, Agnes, Augustine, Dominic, Francis of Assisi, Ignatius Loyola, Gertrude, Catherine of Sienna, Rose of Lima, and Theresa of Avila. [To the right of Christ, "Saints of France"]: Saints Lazarus of Marseilles, Mary-Madalene, Martha, Denis, Martin, Genevieve, Bernard, Louis, Francois de Sales, Vincent de Paul, Marguerite Mary, Jean-Eudes, Madeleine-Sophie Barrat."

Underneath this mosaic mural was a Latin inscription reiterating the meaning behind the nation's gift to the Sacréd Heart of Jesus. "To the Sacréd Heart of Christ, France fervent, penitent, and grateful."

In 1904, architect Lucien Magne was selected to pick up where Rauline had left off. Magne was a graduate of the *Beaux-Arts de Paris*, and like many of his predecessors, he had an architectural background in his family. Like Abadie, Magne studied under, shadowed, and partnered with his father, Auguste Magne, on a number of projects. He was also an employee of the City of Paris' Department of Architecture and was a friend of the celebrated Eugene Viollet-le-Duc, most known for his impressive restorations of the Basilica of Saint-Denis, the Mont Saint Michel, and the Notre-Dame Cathedral. Magne was then hired by the Diocesan Committee as a restoration officer for diocesan buildings, and he was later promoted to diocesan architect of the Autun commune and the city of Poitiers.

The Sacré-Cœur received yet another phenomenal gift about a year into Magne's office. The gift was an opulent, king-sized pipe organ, its centerpiece surmounted by a gold-rimmed Roman numeral clock, tucked under the arms of two winged cherubs. Two wooden strips, each panel featuring the images of different saints in circular frames, were displayed on either side of the centerpiece, much like a belt on the waist of the organ.

The organ is said to have been the last project its illustrious creator, the French organ-builder Aristide Cavaille-Coll, completed before his death. It was equipped with "four keyboards, 78 speaking stops, four sets of 61-note manuals, and 109 ranks extending across the 32-note pedal board." Ironically, the organ was not built with the Sacré-Cœur in mind. On the contrary, it was originally ordered by Baron Albert de L'Espee in 1898 to be installed at the parlor of one of his residences, the Chateau de Ilbarritz in the Pyrenees-Antaliques. The baron treasured the stately, one-of-a-kind organ deeply, but for reasons unknown, he chose to sell the instrument to Charles Mutin, a former apprentice of Cavaille-Coll. Mutin, in turn, sold the organ to the operators of the Sacré-Cœur in 1905, and the organ arrived at the basilica at some point during the following decade.

The Grand Organ was inaugurated by the Sacré-Cœur clergymen in 1910. As the instrument was later declared a historical monument in 1981, only "tenured organists" – a short roster of pianists employed by the basilica – are allowed to play it. Today, this roster consists of Claudine Barthel, Gabriel Marghieri, and Philippe Brandeis.

Around this time, the statues of St. King Louis IX and Joan of Arc were mounted on the narthex underneath the statue of Christ by the portico. Both of these sculptures were shaped by the carving chisels and gouges of sculptor Hippolyte Lefebvre, acclaimed for his work in the *Jardin d'Ete,* the Hotel Elysee Palace, and the Opera de Lille. His tasteful, yet imposing equestrian statues of Louis and Joan are now considered his masterpieces. It was also Lefebvre who sculptured the statues now seen on the High Altar in the central nave of the basilica.

These equestrian sculptures, cast in pure bronze, have now turned sea-foam green, a result of the metal's continuous contact with airborne carbon and sulfur dioxides, but this provides the all-white monument with a bright pop of color. Both figures were portrayed on horseback in full battle regalia. Joan of Arc, however, is seen leaning forward, as if directing her stallion to charge forth, her eyes narrowed with an expression of fierce resolve as she clutches the reins of her horse with one hand and wields her sword in the air with the other. Louis was holding his sword aloft, too, only his fist was wrapped around the blade of his weapon just underneath the hilt, as if he was flaunting a cross. In his other hand, he held up a crown of thorns.

Daniel Stockman's picture of the statue of St. King Louis

The statue of Joan of Arc

The layout of the basilica's crypt was also remodeled during this time. The crypt was home to its own assortment of statues, including: St. Denis; St. Ignatius, the patron saint of Catholic soldiers; St. Francis-Xavier, patron saint of Catholic missions and pilgrimages; and St. Genevieve, the patron saint of Paris. Across the St. Peter Chapel was the Pieta Chapel, which housed a statue of the Blessed Mother, as well as the tombs of Archbishop Guibert and Archbishop Richard, upon which rests the life-size effigies of the deceased cardinals.

The crypt continues to host a collection of relics and treasures, such as the heart of Legentil, which is preserved in an urn, and a special case containing fragments of the "Sacréd Heart of Jesus." Visitors will also find the foundation stone of the basilica in mint condition, as well as blocks of marble engraved with the names of priests and seminary students who lost their lives in the Great Wars. Other treasures include a square of cloth taken from an elaborate golden chasuble (sleeveless outer garment worn by Catholic priests), a stole that once belonged to Pope Leo XIII, and a variety of valuable votive offerings (ex-votos) presented to the basilica's clergymen by pilgrims during Thanksgiving.

Even as the basilica was reaching its final stages, a new generation of Sacré-Cœur critics demonstrated their disapproval of the basilica through a different medium: art. Author Elizabeth Emery discussed some of the anti-Sacré-Cœur art produced during this period: "A Theophile Steinlen lithograph of the Sacré-Cœur, published in the illustrated paper, *L'Assiette au Beurre,* portrays the basilica as an evil pope who dominates Paris by casting his web over it, then drawing it into his bloody clutches...A similar image was displayed on the cover of the anticlerical bulletin, *La Lanterne,* which portrayed the Sacré-Cœur with a demonic priest perched above it and the words '*Voila l'Ennemi!* ('Here is the enemy!') at its base."

The Sacré-Cœur also continued to suffer a spate of anticlerical and anti-Sacré-Cœur laws instituted by Republican opponents. An 1882 decree prohibited all clergymen who belonged to the Sacréd Heart cult from preaching. Next came the 1902 purge of monastic orders across the country, and then the declaration of the separation of church and state three years later.

The basilica, at this stage, was fast becoming one of France's architectural crown jewels, yet its detractors continued to find fault in it. A good portion of the Sacré-Cœur's critics disliked the basilica's use of domes, which they deemed "too foreign" and "pagan-looking." Conservative novelist and essayist Leon Bloy, who paid a visit to the basilica in the early 1900s, accused the Sacré-Cœur's clergymen of "selling the Catholic faith for material gain." He complained, "The Sacré-Cœur Basilica is more of a work of vanity than a work of faith...Everything must be paid for there...It is the heart of Jesus transformed into a boutique."

As it turned out, the condemnation of the Sacré-Cœur was a problem that seemed almost petty given the disastrous events that were brewing on the horizon. The second consecration of the basilica, which was soon to be finished, was scheduled for October 17, 1914, but it was postponed following the grim announcement that France had entered the First World War. The consecration was finally performed by Archbishop of Paris Leon-Adolphe Amette and Cardinal Antonio Vico, Prefect of the Congregation of Rites, on October 16, 1919, about a year after the close of the war. The celebratory Mass was also attended by Jean-Louis Hulot, who would oversee the final phase of the basilica's construction.

In 1922, the basilica's builders installed a beautiful selection of stained glass windows. These arresting art pieces featured patron saints with accompanying Latin inscriptions, Biblical scenes, and refined, yet vibrant geometric patterns containing the emblem of the Sacréd Heart. These works were specially tailored to fit the circular and arch-shaped windows peppered throughout the Sacré-Cœur.

On May 20, 1923, during the Pentecostal celebrations, Sacré-Cœur clerics blessed the *Christ in Majesty* mosaic that adorned the apse of the basilica. Construction, at long last, came to an end in the autumn of 1924.

There is still much debate regarding the total cost of the Sacré-Cœur. Some say the donations over the decades amounted to a whopping $40 million, but according to most sources, the actual figure is closer to the neighborhood of $7-10 million.

Laymen and secular visitors from near and far teemed into the Sacré-Cœur in droves to witness the basilica in its full glory during the early 20th century, but attendance experienced another staggering dip at the start of World War II. Things wouldn't get any better when the Nazis occupied the city in the summer of 1940.

On the evening of April 20-21, 1944, a modest batch of pilgrims convened at the Sacré-Cœur to attend a special overnight Mass of the Perpetual Adoration, as well as to pray for the souls of all those involved in the war. The attendees were well-aware of the risks their presence entailed, but the saintly congregation went on with their prayers and incantations anyway, wholly convinced that they would be shielded by the grace of God. The unshakable faith of these pilgrims, as it turns out, seemed to pay off.

It was on this particular evening that Allied fighter jets unleashed a barrage of 13 bombs over Paris, resulting in the near-complete destruction of the La Chapelle railroad station, which lay just two miles east of the Sacré-Cœur. The impact of the neighboring blasts rocked and shattered several windows of the basilica, but miraculously, everyone inside the basilica remained unscathed. The damaged windows were rebuilt and reinstalled two years later.

Pope John Paul II's first apostolic tour, set in France, culminated in the Sacré-Cœur on June 1, 1980. Hundreds of people huddled together in the audience watched, many of them starstruck, as the pope hobbled into the basilica with his entourage just after the stroke of midnight. He concluded the special celebration with a rousing speech: "We come here to meet the pierced heart for us, from which spring water and blood. It is the redeeming love, which is at the origin of salvation, of our salvation, which is at the origin of the Church...Let us contemplate His burning heart of love for His father, in the fullness of the Holy Spirit. Let us contemplate His infinite love, that of the eternal Son, which leads us to the mystery of God...[Regarding] this mystery of the love of Christ...we are not only called to meditate and contemplate, we are called to take part in the cause. It is the mystery of the Holy Eucharist, the center of our faith, the center of worship, that we give back to the merciful love of Christ manifested in his Sacréd Heart, a mystery that is adored here night and day, in this basilica, which becomes one of those centers from which the love and grace of the Lord radiate mysteriously, but truly..."

Before his departure, John Paul II left the spectators with these final words: "I confess that this visit is a privileged moment for me, and will be so for the rest of my life."

Time has done nothing to dilute the animosity towards the Sacré-Cœur. In fact, the opposition has evolved from heated discourse and artwork to more violent acts of protest. In February 1971, about 200 leftist protesters attempted to storm into and seize the basilica, an aggressive endeavor spearheaded by philosopher Jean Paul-Sartre and filmmaker Jean-Luc Godard. The protesters carried with them self-penned pamphlets that vilified the basilica, claiming that it had been "built upon the bodies of Communards in order to efface that red flag that hard for too long floated over Paris," and distributed them to anyone who would accept a flier.

Three years later, an explosive ripped off a chunk of one of the Sacré-Cœur's five cupolas. The crime was repeated a number of times in the decades that followed, most notably in May 1991, when a bomb scorched part of the basilica's bronze doors. Fortunately, there were no reported injuries.

More recently, on March 20, 2014, vandals defaced the doors and the portico floor of the basilica with hateful slogans. "Come on and stand up, great star hunters," said one cryptic message in dripping, blood-red spray-paint. "Neither God, nor master, nor state," read another. "Set fire to all chapels."

Be that as it may, the rector of the Sacré-Cœur urges people to pay no heed to the words and actions of the basilica's disparagers, and to look to the domes of the irreplaceable landmark and be reminded of the basilica's true meaning and message of hope: "At the top of the dome[s], the basilica lantern is lit every night, showing that there is always somebody praying in this sanctuary. It shines like a lighthouse to give hope, strength, and courage to all who see it..."

Online Resources

Other books about French history by Charles River Editors

Other books about the Sacré-Cœur on Amazon

Bibliography

Auvillain, A. (2018, January 4). Tourists, pilgrims find sisters' welcome at Montmartre's Sacré-Cœur. Retrieved May 15, 2019, from http://www.globalsistersreport.org/news/ministry-spirituality/tourists-pilgrims-find-sisters-welcome-montmartres-sacré-Cœur-51126

Brigstocke, J. (2016). *The Life of the City: Space, Humour, and the Experience of Truth in Fin-de-siècle Montmartre*. Routledge.

Cole, N. L., Ph.D. (2019, February 5). What You Need to Know About the Paris Commune of 1871. Retrieved May 15, 2019, from https://www.thoughtco.com/paris-commune-4147849

Cunningham, J. M. (2011, June 15). Druid. Retrieved May 15, 2019, from https://www.britannica.com/topic/Druid

Editors, A. P. (1991, May 28). Bomb Damages Door of Sacré Cœur. Retrieved May 15, 2019, from https://apnews.com/a39a8ad60544734b67fb9430944444c7

Editors, A. P. (2010, December). Basilique du Sacré-Cœur. Retrieved May 15, 2019, from http://architectureofparis.blogspot.com/2010/12/basilique-du-Sacré-cur.html

Editors, B. S. (2015). The Seventh Persecution, Under Decius, A.D. 249. Retrieved May 15, 2019, from https://www.biblestudytools.com/history/foxs-book-of-martyrs/the-seventh-persecution-under-decius-a-d-249.html

Editors, C. I. (2012, October 16). Oct 16 – St Margaret Mary Alacoque (1647-90) visionary. Retrieved May 15, 2019, from https://www.catholicireland.net/saintoftheday/st-margaret-mary-alacoque-1647-90-visionary/

Editors, C. T. (2017). Basilique du Sacré-Cœur de Montmartre. Retrieved May 15, 2019, from https://www.cntraveler.com/activities/paris/basilique-du-Sacré-Cœur-de-montmartre

Editors, D. W. (2018, April 19). Top 10 fun facts about the Sacré-Cœur. Retrieved May 15, 2019, from https://www.discoverwalks.com/blog/top-10-fun-facts-about-the-Sacré-Cœur/

Editors, D. W. (2019, February 28). Paul Abadie, the architect of Sacré Cœur. Retrieved May 15, 2019, from https://www.discoverwalks.com/blog/paul-abadie-the-architect-of-Sacré-Cœur/

Editors, E. T. (2011). History of Sacré Cœur Basilica and Montmartre in Paris. Retrieved May 15, 2019, from https://www.eutouring.com/history_Sacré_Cœur_basilica.html

Editors, E. (2016). LAISNÉ Charles, Jean. Retrieved May 15, 2019, from http://elec.enc.sorbonne.fr/architectes/303

Editors, F. T. (2013, June 16). The Bells of Annecy. Retrieved May 15, 2019, from https://www.francetoday.com/culture/made_in_france/the_bells_of_annecy/

Editors, F. M. (2017, June 4). Discover the village of Montmartre in Paris. Retrieved May 15, 2019, from https://frenchmoments.eu/montmartre-paris/

Editors, F. P. (2017, May 14). June 17, 1889: Death of philanthropist Alexandre Legentil, initiator of the building of the Sacréd Heart. Retrieved May 15, 2019, from https://www.france-pittoresque.com/spip.php?article14495

Editors, F. W. (2018, December 20). Alexandre Legentil. Retrieved May 15, 2019, from https://fr.wikipedia.org/wiki/Alexandre_Legentil

Editors, F. W. (2018, July 8). Honoré Daumet. Retrieved May 15, 2019, from https://fr.wikipedia.org/wiki/Honoré_Daumet

Editors, F. W. (2018, March 17). Henri-Pierre Rauline. Retrieved May 15, 2019, from https://fr.wikipedia.org/wiki/Henri-Pierre_Rauline

Editors, F. M. (2019, April 8). Top 10 Facts about the Sacré-Cœur, Paris. Retrieved May 15, 2019, from https://frenchmoments.eu/top-10-facts-about-the-Sacré-Cœur-paris/

Editors, F. M. (2019, April 17). Sacré-Cœur Basilica, Paris. Retrieved May 15, 2019, from https://frenchmoments.eu/Sacré-Cœur-basilica-paris/

Editors, F. W. (2019, May 15). Basilique du Sacré-Cœur de Montmartre. Retrieved May 15, 2019, from https://fr.wikipedia.org/wiki/Basilique_du_Sacré-Cœur_de_Montmartre

Editors, F. W. (2019, May 8). Lucien Magne. Retrieved May 15, 2019, from https://fr.wikipedia.org/wiki/Lucien_Magne

Editors, H. H. (2018). Sacré Cœur Historical Facts and Pictures. Retrieved May 15, 2019, from https://www.thehistoryhub.com/Sacré-Cœur-facts-pictures.htm

Editors, I. P. (2012). Armagnacs and Burgundians. Retrieved May 15, 2019, from https://www.infoplease.com/encyclopedia/history/modern-europe/france/armagnacs-and-burgundians

Editors, I. C. (2018, June 6). Speech of Saint John Paul II to the Sacréd Heart of Montmartre. Retrieved May 15, 2019, from https://www.infocatho.fr/discours-de-saint-jean-paul-ii-au-Sacré-Cœur-de-montmartre/

Editors, J. F. (2016). Interesting facts about the Sacré Cœur. Retrieved May 15, 2019, from http://justfunfacts.com/interesting-facts-about-the-Sacré-Cœur/

Editors, M. M. (2011, September 12). Charles VI of France. Retrieved May 15, 2019, from http://madmonarchs.guusbeltman.nl/madmonarchs/charles6/charles6_bio.htm

Editors, O. B. (2012, March 26). Paris Commune formed. Retrieved May 15, 2019, from https://blog.oup.com/2012/03/paris-commune-formed/

Editors, P. L. (2012). Sacré Cœur Basilica in Montmartre. Retrieved May 15, 2019, from https://www.parislogue.com/planning-a-trip/Sacré-Cœur-basilica-in-montmarte/

Editors, P. I. (2019, March 17). 5 Things You Didn't Know About the Sacré-Cœur. Retrieved May 15, 2019, from http://plug-inn.fr/uncategorized/five-things-you-didnt-know-about-the-Sacré-Cœur/

Editors, R. T. (2014, March 20). 'F**k tourism': Vandals deface Paris' Sacré Cœur basilica. Retrieved May 15, 2019, from https://www.rt.com/news/Sacré-Cœur-paris-vandalised-989/

Editors, R. (2019, May 13). Montmartre. Retrieved May 15, 2019, from https://www.revolvy.com/page/Montmartre

Editors, R. (2019, February 27). Margaret Mary Alacoque. Retrieved May 15, 2019, from https://www.revolvy.com/page/Margaret-Mary-Alacoque

Editors, R. (2019, March 31). Decian persecution. Retrieved May 15, 2019, from https://www.revolvy.com/page/Decian-persecution

Editors, R. (2019, January 3). Paul Abadie. Retrieved May 15, 2019, from https://www.revolvy.com/page/Paul-Abadie

Editors, S. D. (2012). Sacré-Cœur, Paris. Retrieved May 15, 2019, from http://www.Sacréd-destinations.com/france/paris-Sacré-Cœur

Editors, S. C. (2014). LA SAVOYARDE. Retrieved May 15, 2019, from http://www.Sacré-Cœur-montmartre.com/francais/histoire-et-visite/article/la-savoyarde

Editors, S. C. (2015). CHARLES DE FOUCAULD ET LA BASILIQUE. Retrieved May 15, 2019, from http://www.Sacré-Cœur-montmartre.com/francais/spiritualite-du-Sacré-Cœur/les-saints-de-la-basilique/le-bienheureux-charles-de-foucauld/article/charles-de-foucauld-et-la

Editors, S. C. (2016). MONTMARTRE, THE "MOUNT OF MARTYRS". Retrieved May 15, 2019, from http://www.Sacré-Cœur-montmartre.com/english/history-and-visit/article/montmartre-the-mount-of-martyrs

Editors, S. C. (2016). FOUR STEPS TO LEARN MORE ABOUT SACRÉ-CŒUR. Retrieved May 15, 2019, from http://www.Sacré-Cœur-montmartre.com/english/visit-and-audio-guide/article/four-steps-to-learn-more-about

Editors, S. C. (2016). VOCATION OF THE BASILICA. Retrieved May 15, 2019, from http://www.Sacré-Cœur-montmartre.com/english/night-adoration/article/vocation

Editors, S. C. (2016). THE CRYPT. Retrieved May 15, 2019, from http://www.Sacré-Cœur-montmartre.com/english/history-and-visit/article/the-crypt

Editors, S. C. (2017). THE ORIGIN OF THE CONSTRUCTION OF THE BASILICA, A "NATIONAL VOW". Retrieved May 15, 2019, from http://www.Sacré-Cœur-montmartre.com/english/history-and-visit/article/the-origin-of-the-construction-of

Editors, S. C. (2017). ARCHITECTURE. Retrieved May 15, 2019, from http://www.Sacré-Cœur-montmartre.com/english/history-and-visit/article/architecture

Editors, S. C. (2018). THE APSE MOSAIC. Retrieved May 15, 2019, from http://www.Sacré-Cœur-montmartre.com/english/history-and-visit/article/the-apse-mosaic

Editors, S. C. (2018). THE GRAND ORGAN. Retrieved May 15, 2019, from
http://www.Sacré-Cœur-montmartre.com/english/history-and-visit/article/the-grand-organ

Editors, T. C. (2010). Novena to St. Denis. Retrieved May 15, 2019, from
https://www.catholickingdom.com/Cathedral/Prayer/novenas/St_Denis.html

Editors, T. C. (2017, February 28). Parisian Citizen Proposes Demolition of the Sacré-Cœur, "
Insult to the Memory of the Commune". Retrieved May 15, 2019, from
https://tendancecoatesy.wordpress.com/2017/02/28/parisian-citizen-proposes-demolition-of-the-
Sacré-Cœur-insult-to-the-memory-of-the-commune/

Editors, T. F. (2018, February 6). Montmartre - Mont des Martyrs. Retrieved May 15, 2019,
from http://www.travelfranceonline.com/montmartre-abbey-sanctum-martyrium-crypt/#

Editors, U. T. (2012). Story of Saint Denis. Retrieved May 15, 2019, from
https://uk.tourisme93.com/basilica/saint-denis-martyred.html

Editors, V. C. (2018). Sacré-Cœur. Retrieved May 15, 2019, from
https://www.aviewoncities.com/paris/SacréCœur.htm

Editors, W. P. (2011). Sacré-Cœur. Retrieved May 15, 2019, from
https://www.whatparis.com/Sacré-Cœur.html

Editors, W. S. (2014). Sacré-Cœur Basilica , Paris. Retrieved May 15, 2019, from
https://www.worldsiteguides.com/Sacré-Cœur-basilica/

Editors, W. A. (2015). Architectural Buildings Of The World: Basilica Du Sacré-Cœur De
Montmartre. Retrieved May 15, 2019, from https://www.worldatlas.com/articles/architectural-
buildings-of-the-world-basilica-du-Sacré-Cœur-de-montmartre.html

Editors, W. (2017, November 4). Hippolyte Lefèbvre. Retrieved May 15, 2019, from
https://en.wikipedia.org/wiki/Hippolyte_Lefèbvre

Emery, E. (2001). *Romancing the Cathedral: Gothic Architecture in Fin-de-Siecle French
Culture*. SUNY Press.

Gee, L. (2018, January 7). 10 Fun Facts on the Sacré-Cœur in Paris. Retrieved May 15, 2019,
from https://traveltips.usatoday.com/10-fun-SacréCœur-paris-106883.html

Hildebrandt, V. (2018). Sacré-Cœur. Retrieved May 15, 2019, from
https://www.organsparisaz4.vhhil.nl/Sacré Cœur.htm

Jonas, R. A. (1993, Autumn). Monument as Ex-Voto, Monument as Historiosophy: The Basilica of Sacré-Cœur. Retrieved May 15, 2019, from https://www.jstor.org/stable/286877?seq=1#page_scan_tab_contents

Lotha, G. (2018, September 27). Commune of Paris. Retrieved May 15, 2019, from https://www.britannica.com/event/Commune-of-Paris-1871

Malik, S., & Davenport, C. (2018, January 17). Mythbusting Ancient Rome: Cruel and unusual punishment. Retrieved May 15, 2019, from https://theconversation.com/mythbusting-ancient-rome-cruel-and-unusual-punishment-87939

Nadeau, S. (2016, August 23). THE SACRÉ CŒUR AND ITS PAGAN ORIGINS. Retrieved May 15, 2019, from https://www.solosophie.com/Sacré-Cœur/

O'Riordan, M. (2017). Saint Therese of the Child Jesus of the Holy Face. Retrieved May 15, 2019, from http://www.thereseoflisieux.org/my-blog-about-st-therese/tag/basilique-du-Sacré-Cœur

Pirie, M. (2016). THE PARIS COMMUNE OF 1871. Retrieved May 15, 2019, from https://www.adamsmith.org/blog/the-paris-commune-of-1871

Tikkanen, A. (2009, October 13). Saint Denis. Retrieved May 15, 2019, from https://www.britannica.com/biography/Saint-Denis

Wasson, D. L. (2014, February 12). Decius. Retrieved May 15, 2019

Free Books by Charles River Editors

We have brand new titles available for free most days of the week. To see which of our titles are currently free, click on this link.

Discounted Books by Charles River Editors

We have titles at a discount price of just 99 cents everyday. To see which of our titles are currently 99 cents, click on this link.

Made in the USA
Monee, IL
16 July 2022

99823225R00033